How Obama Won

How Obama Won
by
Earl Ofari Hutchinson

MID DLE
PASS AGE
PRESS

How Obama Won

Printed in the United States

Published by
Middle Passage Press
5517 Secrest Drive
Los Angeles, California 90043

Designed by Alan Bell

Publisher's Cataloging-in-Publication
(Provided by Quality Books, Inc.)

Hutchinson, Earl Ofari.
    How Obama won / by Earl Ofari Hutchinson.
    p. cm.
    Includes index.
    LCCN: 2008910732
    ISBN-13: 978-1439219294
    ISBN-10: 143921929X
1. Obama, Barack. 2. Presidents—United States—Election—2008. 3. African
Americans—Politics and government. 4. United States—Politics and
government—2001- I. Title.
JK526 2008.H88 2009   324.973'0931
                                       QBI08-600333

Table of Contents

How Obama Won

Prescript

At an election night campaign stop during the Iowa Democratic caucus on January 3, 2008 Democratic presidential candidate Barack Obama shouted to cheering supporters that it was time for change and Americans want that change. America's first major African-American candidate for the presidency had just won a smash victory in the caucus. It proved to be a prophetic shout. Eight months and a presidential election win later on November 4, he told an Election Night throng in Chicago's Grant Park that his election was stunning proof that America is a place where all things are possible.

Obama's election was indeed the fulfillment of the impossible dream, a symbol of racial and democratic progress, and a historic epoch making event all in one. But that was the glamour spin. Obama's win was not a smooth, straight line win. The win was filled with twists and turns, crises, reverses, political soul searches, hard political bargaining and fence mending with political foes, and with strategies and tactics devised to break down and break through racial barriers and biases. Obama's path to the White House was made possible by a smooth, well oiled, well-financed organization that was a master-piece of skill and organization.

This was crucial for Obama since there was no incumbent in the White House in 2008 for him to run against. The President who would leave office would depart with an approval rating that ranked with the worst of the bottom rung presidents.

In the end, though, Obama triumphed because he convincingly made the case to the American people that he was the one who was best for America. *How Obama Won* tells the story of how and why he triumphed. *How Obama Won* is based on political analyst Earl Ofari Hutchinson's *Huffington Post* columns which meticulously examined the forces and events that shaped Obama's historic victory.

How Obama Won the White House

A Pew Research Poll Center poll in May 2008 found that "inspiring, "fresh," "change," and "visionary" were not the words that voters said best described Democratic presidential contender Barack Obama. The word was "inexperienced." Republican presidential rival John McCain made this and the boast that he was the best on national security, the terrorist fight and defense preparedness his attack mantra against Obama.

Obama had to parry the attack by turning the table and proclaiming that his lack of national and especially international experience was a positive. He stated that he'd bring fresh ideas and approaches to statecraft in order to replace the old, tired, and failed polices of recent times. But that was not enough. He had to choose and choose carefully to find a vice presidential running mate who was every bit as hard nosed on national security, the war on terrorism and defense preparedness that McCain claimed to be. Then he had to convince voters that he would back up his pledge to bring an honorable and workable end to the Iraq war.

But it was still Bush and the GOP's domestic fumbles that were potentially his biggest selling point. He had repeatedly reminded voters they should be mad at Bush and the GOP for the bungle of the economy, his draconian tax giveaway to the wealthy and corporate interests, his gut of environmental and civil liberties protections, and his Medicare prescription drug benefit bill lined the pockets of pharmaceutical companies and eroded Medicare coverage and protections. He had to adeptly remind women's groups that the GOP would continue to wage a relentless war against abortion rights and to remind gay groups that top GOP politicians were staunch opponents of gay marriage, and were likely to continue to fight hard against stronger civil rights protections for gays.

However, that was not enough. He had to make the ringing call by the Democrats for party unity more than a feel-good, politically correct self-assuring call. That meant repairing the deep polarization among Democratic voters, or more particularly, the hardliners who backed his Democratic presidential opponent Hillary Clinton and were wary if not hostile to him. He had to make an all out effort to convince white blue collar and rural voters that an Obama White House would aggressively battle against soaring gas prices, home foreclosures, job losses, plant closures, the erosion of farm supports and to implement affordable health care. He also had to convince these voters that a McCain White House wouldn't do these things.

He had to make an equally aggressive effort to convince Latinos that an Obama White House would just as forcefully fight for immigration reform and affordable health care. In addition, they had to believe that a McCain White House wouldn't.

Obama had to turn the campaign for the White House into a holy crusade among black and Latino voters. The enthusiasm of black voters for Obama and Latino voters for Clinton was sky high in the primaries and the numbers that turned out were near record setting. The bellwether for that was Obama's smash victory in the South Carolina primary in January, 2008. More than a half million Democrats voted. That was nearly twice the Democratic turnout of 2004 and almost 20 percent higher than the Republican vote the week before. Blacks make up more than half of the Democratic vote in the state. In California, Latinos make up nearly 30 percent of the voters and had a higher than average turnout in the Super Tuesday primary in February, 2008.

He had to make sure those near record numbers that flooded the polls in the primaries flooded the polls in near record or better yet record numbers on Election Day, November 4.

Obama had to convince a significant number of swing state independent voters that he was the "real change" alternative to McCain in handling the war, the economy, health care, immigration and energy issues, and was centrist enough to convince them that he is as tough on terrorism and as big an advocate of a strong military as McCain.

Most importantly, he had to convince a significant percent of white voters, who make up three quarters of American voters, that his campaign and candidacy was transformative. That meant that it was a broad issues appeal, race neutral campaign, non sectarian, and all inclusive. In other words, he and his campaign was an every person's campaign with something for everyone—small town, rural, big city, blue collar white, gay, women, Christian evangelicals, blacks, Latinos, Asians, and Native-Americans.

This was a tall, but very doable, order. That, and a timely collapse of the economy, and the deep, pervasive and all consuming fury at President Bush by millions of Americans, was the only way that Barack Obama could win the White House. The political stars aligned neatly for him to become the 44th president of the United States.

Book 1
Jumpstarting the Campaign

CHAPTER 1

Win Iowa or Lose the Democratic Nomination

I n December, 2007 former W. Bush political operative Karl Rove put it bluntly to then Democratic presidential contender Barack Obama; win Iowa or lose the Democratic nomination. A month before Rove's admonition, Obama's wife, Michelle, told her hubby pretty much the same thing; win Iowa or lose the nomination. Obama moved fast to distance himself from his wife's blanket assertion about Iowa. He assured reporters that Iowa was only one state and that a loss there wouldn't spell doom for his campaign. But even as he downplayed his wife's remark, and was publicly mute about Rove's Iowa rejoinder, he knew better.

From the moment Obama stood on the steps of the state capitol building in Springfield, Illinois on February 10, 2007 and announced the launch of his "Dream campaign" he knew Iowa was big, very big, so big that he dumped more money into his campaign there, opened more field offices there than Democratic presidential rivals Hillary Clinton and John Edwards, and virtually camped out in the state. A win there certainly would give any candidate a rocket launch boost in public and party standing, much media attention, and potentially piles of campaign money. Iowa did much for Democratic presidential contender John Kerry who was a decided underdog in 2004 against then frontrunner Howard Dean going into the Iowa primary. Kerry won Iowa and bagged the nomination, and Dean bungled it. Dean quickly became a campaign laughingstock and a bare campaign 2004 footnote.

An Iowa win wouldn't do that for Obama. But a win or a solid showing would give a hint whether he could get a majority or at least a significant percent of whites to vote for him. Iowa is one of the whitest and most rural states in the union. In 2008, white voters made up more than ninety percent of the state's voters.

That posed a possibility and a pitfall. He would have to convince the voters that he could deliver on his promises on health care, revving up the economy, labor protections, wind down the Iraq War, and wage a tough war on terrorism. He then hoped and prayed that enough of them would buy his message, and not succumb to the dreaded voting booth conversion on Election Day. The voting booth conversion is the alleged penchant of some white voters to swear to pollsters and interviewers they are absolutely color-blind when it comes to black candidates, and that the only thing they judge the candidate on is their record and qualifications. And then once in the quiet and very private confines of the voting booth, develop collective amnesia and vote for the white candidate.

Voting booth conversion was widely thought to spell doom for some black candidates who were thought to be shoo-in winners in head to head contests against white opponents, and then later go down to crashing defeat on Election Day. Whether that was true or not, it was still a genuine concern for black candidates running head to head against white opponents where the majority of voters were white.

Polls in the state showed Obama would either win Iowa or make a big showing there, and the odds were good that the polls were accurate. He was riding what appeared to be a genuine crest of public goodwill, and mixed with his likeability, personal appeal, charisma, and media warmth, that should have been enough to convince a sufficient number of white Iowa voters that he was a genuine change agent and could bring the directional shift that millions of American voters said they desperately craved to shift away from Bush's disastrous domestic and foreign policies.

While Iowa was important for Obama, it was also an aberration among the heartland states. It's moderately Democratic leaning, has a mild populist tradition, and voters are known to be independent on candidates and issues. These are the exact opposite traits of the other heartland states which are traditionalist, deeply conservative, and rock solid Republican. No white Democratic presidential candidate had managed to crack them in elections going back to the 1980s, including Bill Clinton. He didn't win one heartland state in 1996.

These states were also a good gauge of whether Obama could

really convince millions of white voters, especially white male voters, who still make up nearly forty percent of the country's voters and have been the path to the White House for Nixon, Reagan, Bush Sr., and W. Bush   . Clinton who slightly dented the GOP lock on the South had to deftly pirouette and convince the voters that he was a safe alternative to the GOP candidate and that he would not pander to special interest for example minorities and women.

Even if Obama were able to speak the language of white voters in Iowa, and persuade them that he was not a black presidential candidate, but a color neutral presidential candidate, that wouldn't automatically lift the clouds of suspicion about him in the other heartland states.

Still a win in Iowa would give Obama's dream campaign an adrenalin shot, and convince more of the Democratic Party leaders that he, not Hillary, was the party's "go to" candidate. As it turned out, Obama's breakthrough win in Iowa did just that and set him firmly on the tough path that still lay ahead of him.

CHAPTER 2

The Four Lessons of Iowa

D emocratic presidential candidate Barack Obama proclaimed to cheering supporters at a campaign stop in Iowa in early January, 2008 that it was time for change and Americans wanted that change. This was lesson number one in Obama's smash caucus victory. Iowans and Americans wanted, no, craved change. They were fed up with the lies, deceit, corruption, cronyism, politics for sale, war mongering, political paralysis and bungling along with the economic wreckage wreaked by Bush, Congress, and legions of "on the make" politicians. Though Obama could hardly be considered a maverick, who challenged the establishment elected official, at the very least, he was an energetic, fresh, new face on the national scene and he was savvy enough to figure out how to talk the talk of change. That was enough for packs of voters.

The second lesson of Iowa was that money couldn't always buy a political win. Republican presidential contender Mitt Romney outspent the other Republican opponents by more than six to one in the state. It didn't help. In fact, it hurt the money candidates. It reinforced the notion that if politicians and their corporate backers spread enough cash around they can buy anything. That idea repels millions of Americans. They repeatedly say that money and corruption go hand in hand and are twin political evils. Americans say that's exactly why the political system is so screwed up. They are sick of watching the parade of fat cat lobbyists and corporate bigwigs buy and sell politicians and elections, and then watch as those bought and paid for politicians give away the company store to those same interests when they torpedo affordable health care, erode labor protections, pour billions into bloated defense spending, and shove through economy draining tax cuts for the super rich and corporations. Many people felt Obama was the candidate who would reverse this trend.

Lesson number three of Iowa was that race didn't always matter the most to white voters. Iowa is one of the whitest and most rural states in the nation. Yet, white voters were able to strap on color blind lenses and punch the ticket for Obama. This was historic. It was a good sign that many more whites than ever before were willing to truly look past race, and back up the promise they repeatedly made to interviewers and pollsters (but didn't always keep in the past) that they would vote based on the competence and qualifications of a candidate not their race. This was not smoking gun proof that race still didn't matter in politics but it was a good sign that it may no longer be the thing that matters most with an increasing number of white voters.

Lesson number four was that the national media's turn off to Hillary Clinton paid off, and it paid off big. The Hillary media meltdown deeply convinced far too many voters that Hillary was a classic political pandering and corporate shill, and that a vote for her was a vote for the status quo. This again reaffirmed the power and dominance of big media and its ability to spin, shade, and massage public opinion to suit its ends.

The presidential election was far from over. After Obama's Iowa win, there were more primaries ahead for him, and more tough battles. A slip, a misstep, or a scandal could have been fatal to Obama. But Iowa clearly marked him as the candidate to beat.

CHAPTER 3

It Was Still the Economy Stupid

I n a two minute nationally paid campaign broadcast billed as a "presidential style" talk to the nation in mid September, 2008, Obama talked about one issue, and one issue only, the economy. There wasn't much new in his talk. But it really didn't have to be anything new. Polls by then showed the economy; or rather the train wreck of the economy was really the only thing on voter's minds.

Obama again vowed to cut taxes for the middle-class, clean up Wall Street's mess, and create lots of jobs for everybody. He aimed to firmly seize back the high ground on the defining issue of economic misery of the middle and working class. That is the Bush-GOP caused economic misery. This was widely regarded as Obama's surefire ticket to the White House. It was a play on the old political truism that "it's the economy stupid that wins or loses presidential elections."

From day one of campaign 2008 the enshrined article of political faith was that voters were so furious at Bush for causing massive plant closings, farm failures, corporate bungling, fraud and corruption, the housing collapse, soaring gas prices, and the wholesale flight of jobs to the far corners of the planet, that all a Democratic presidential contender had to do to win was pass the breath test on Election Day. Of course, it wasn't quite that simple. The economy has broken presidents, but a lot depends on when the economy breaks and how bad voters perceive the break will affect them personally. In a look at how six of eight presidents fared since 1948 when the economy hit the skids or appeared to skid, the scorecard for presidents winning and losing because of economic woes was a draw. Three were beaten and three beat back their challengers. It came down to whether voters really perceived that their economic plight, or rather pain, would show no sign of a cure if they kept the incumbent in office.

Both Republican and Democratic presidents have won and lost even when there was widespread public unease over the economy and when many voters believed things wouldn't get any better. The presidents who won had to do one crucial thing in the face of rising unemployment, recession, inflation, and public grumbles. They had to assure a majority of voters that things would and could get better for the voters if they stayed in the White House and that their opponent couldn't do any better.

That combination of real and voter perceived economic woe helped sink Presidents Gerald Ford and Bush Sr. It helped and hurt Carter. It helped when the economy went bad for Ford in 1976 allow-ing Carter to win a narrow victory over Ford. The trick is that voters have to think things will get worse, in which case the challenger to a sitting president must reinforce public dread that things will indeed get worse.

Four years later, when the economy went bad for Carter, Reagan won in a near landslide. The exact reverse was true for Reagan and Bill Clinton. Reagan's supply side economics and big tax cuts were credited with igniting a mid-1980s economic boom. Clinton's tax hike, deficit reduction program, and investment stimulus program, was credited with turning a record deficit into a record surplus and adding millions of new jobs to the rolls.

As Reagan's vice president, Bush Sr. benefited from his economic policies. In 1988, he won the election. Four years later, when things turned sour he lost. The more important thing is not just a bad economy but at what point the economy turns bad in the life of the administration, and the public perception of whether things will get better or worse. The downturn for Bush Sr. came during the last two years of his term. Voters are much more likely to blame and punish a president if they go to the polls with economic doubts fresh in their minds.

Bush Sr.'s history then did not repeat itself with W. Bush in the 2004 election. Even though unemployment was high and economic growth, as Democrats gleefully noted, was slower than during Clinton's second term, the Clinton bar was impossibly high to match anyway. By all economic standards, his economic track record was the best of any of the last five presidents. Even by his inflated standard, and despite the industrial erosion in some sections of the country, during the last two years of Bush's first term, overall unemployment and economic growth still slightly improved.

This was the powerful spur that Bush used to spin news, even bad economic news, into a gain. He solemnly pledged there would be more economic goodies for voters if he was reelected. If the economic negatives had hit harder in his last two years, as it did with his father, it would have been Democratic presidential John Kerry's ticket to the White House.

In 2008, Democrat's got the break of a presidential lifetime, and the crash didn't hit in the last two years of the party in power's tenure but the last two months before Election Day. Obama relentlessly hammered that point home.

He painted a stark, grim and scary picture for workers and the middle class that the crash was Bush's doing and by extension McCain's doing. He reinforced the idea that things would only get worse if McCain was elected.

Obama directly linked the perceived failure of Bush to right the nation's economic ship to McCain. That entailed several things. The first was to publicly itemize McCain's plan to deal with the sub prime housing crisis, create more jobs, and hold down inflation. Obama then had to tie McCain's economic plan into Bush's disastrous tax cuts. Finally, he had to make the case that to stimulate the economy McCain would rely on the standard Republican formula of more and bigger tax cuts to major corporations, and the wealthy. Those policies would result in still bigger deficits, the prospect of even greater inflation and a more intense recession.

There was nothing really new in this political one-upmanship. The history of presidential elections showed that a Democrat presidential candidate had to do everything possible to make voters believe the vast majority of workers, middle class and the poor would be better off under a Democratic administration instead of a Republican administration. In 2008, it was Obama's turn to try to make voters believe that Republican economic policy would not promote recovery and economic security but would increase economic pain for millions of wage earners.

Obama was able to do that and that moved him one giant step further down the path to the White House. After all, it was still the economy, stupid.

CHAPTER 4

Team Obama's Money Game Changer

September 15, 2008 was a rare day for Democratic Presidential contender Barack Obama and Republican rival John McCain. They both lambasted the greedy and corrupt (to use their words) Wall Street wheeler dealers for wreaking financial mayhem and pain on Main Street. The tough talk grabbed headlines and made the two contenders sound like the proverbial men on the white horses populists ready to take on the Wall Street greed merchants.

There was one thing, however, conspicuously missing from their Wall Street assault. They didn't name the names of the greedy and corrupt executives or the malfeasant companies they blamed for causing the pain and suffering. In the days after the financial meltdown, they kept up their Wall Street attack, yet they still mentioned no names.

This was no politically absent minded oversight. The prime culprits in the financial mess were prime players on Team Obama and Team McCain. They were prime team players even after the roaring financial Tsushima hit.

Team McCain's Wall Street players bundled nearly $80 million in campaign contributions. That was nearly 60 percent of his campaign funds.

This was the very partial list of Team McCain Wall Street Team players all of whom have been deeply implicated in dubious subprime lending, stock swaps, trading and buys, credit manipulations, and influence peddling:

Citigroup, Inc.	$145,050
Blank Rome LLP	$141,400
Greenberg Traurig	$129,987
Merrill Lynch	$119,675
Goldman Sachs	$111,050
IDT Corp	$80,150
Pinnacle West Capital	$77,850
Bank of New York Mellon	$74,000
JP Morgan Chase & Co.	$72,100
Credit Suisse Group	$63,350
Lehman Brothers	$61,450
Bridgewater Assoc	$58,300
Cisco Systems	$56,850
Wachovia Corp.	$52,100
Morgan Stanley	$51,950

In elections past that would have been more than enough to put the GOP presidential contender at a severe disadvantage if not outright seal an election victory for the Democrat. Republican presidents and presidential contenders since the Reagan years have enjoyed a huge fund gathering corporate fed and friendly fund gap over Democrats.

This time things were different, much different. Team Obama matched and in some cases exceeded Team McCain in the mad dash to bundle cash from Wall Street In a hard nosed campaign back speech in San Antonio, Texas in February, 2008 Obama blasted a top executive of a major sub-prime lender for getting an obscene severance package while millions were facing home foreclosures. The inference was that Obama would crackdown on sub-prime lending offenders.

However, Obama's campaign finance chair was Penny Pritzker. She was the former CEO of the defunct Superior Bank. The bank was knee deep in the sub-prime lending scam that put thousands of mostly poor and minority home borrowers in Chicago in deep hock. The Obama campaign responded to queries about her key money involvement with the campaign by reminding people that she was not charged or accused of any criminal wrongdoing, and that the Pritzker family entered into a voluntary settlement and agreed to pay the government $460 million to defray its losses. Pritzker stayed and continued to bundle millions from her banking and financial sources for the Obama campaign. This proved crucial to the off the charts fundraising record that Obama ultimately set.

Pritzker was only one of Team Obama Wall Street players. Here was a partial list of the others:

Theodore Janulis—Bundler (over $50,000) & Lehman Brothers Head of Global Mortgages

Francisco Borges—Bundler (over $50,000) & Chairman of Landmark Partners a private equity real estate firm.

Nadja Fidelia—Bundler (over $50,000) & Managing Director of Lehman Brothers

Michael Froman—Bundler (over $50,000) & Managing Director of Citigroup

David Heller—Bundler (over $200,000) & Managing Director of Goldman Sachs

J. Michael Schell—Bundler (over $100,000) & Managing Director at Citigroup

Jim Torrey—Bundler (over $200,000) & founder of the Torrey Funds—Hedge Funds

Todd Williams—Bundler (over $50,000) & Managing Director Goldman Sachs & the Real Estate Council

Tom Wheeler, Capital Partners, $100,000

Stanley O'Neal, former Chairman of Merrill Lynch $4,600

Brad Morrice, the former CEO and President of the imploded sub-prime lender, New Century Financial $4,600

Dozens of Lehman Brothers Executives, such as CEO Richard Fuld, and President Joseph Gregory kicked in tens of thousands to Obama's campaign.

Eric Schwartz, the co-head of Goldman-Sachs Global Asset Management helped raise over $50,000.

Robert Wolf, the CEO of UBS Americas helped raise more than $200,000

Louis Susman, the Chairman of a Citibank subsidiary raised roughly the same amount.

Team Obama had the right to take or bundle money from any

legitimate source, including Wall Street and that gave him the crushing financial edge over McCain, who kept his pledge to adhere to the campaign public financing maximum allowed. The public financing system entitles the major party nominees to take up to $84 million of taxpayer funds for their campaign.

In return, candidates agree not to take private donations, so they're effectively limited to the $84 million. Individuals are limited to giving $2,300 to their candidate per election cycle.

There were two potential problems with Obama's Wall Street team members and heavy money flow. One problem is that the heavy cash from them could make it hard to believe that his tough talk about Wall Street greed, corruption and even crackdowns was anything more than fiery campaign talk.

The other problem was that the record amount he raised outside the public campaign financing system raised the bar so high that future presidential contenders would be expected to raise stratospheric sums to be competitive. That would subvert the very purpose of public election funding, namely to ensure a fair, competitive and level election playing field. This would further ensure that politicians weren't for sale to mega-dollar corporate and banking special interests. The saving grace was that a significant percent of Obama's money take did come from small donors. This showed that a candidate with an inspired message of change could attract crucial financial support from regular citizens as well.

In the end, the money, whether it came from the super-rich and corporate America, or the little people, was the political game changer for Obama.

Book 2
Race and the Campaign

CHAPTER 5

The Catch-22 Black Vote

In exit polls before the May 6, 2008 North Carolina Democratic presidential primary nearly a quarter of black voters flatly said race was the biggest factor in their vote. Obviously that meant race motivated them to vote for Obama. The percent of them who said race drove them to Obama dwarfed the percent of whites who said race was a factor, and presumably that meant they voted for Clinton.

The white and black racial divide was virtually frozen and predictable for Clinton and Obama from the start of their primary battles. More than ninety percent of blacks backed Obama and the overwhelming majority of whites backed Clinton. But, his black support was the most compelling and problematic issue for him and the Democrats.

Black Obama supporters treated has candidacy as a virtual

messianic holy calling. Black church leaders came close to a dive off the deep end by shouting out his name with that of Jesus. Obama furor among blacks was so great that the considerable number of black Clinton supporters were bullied and harangued as racial traitors. Former BET founder and billionaire businessman Bob Johnson also took heavy heat from many blacks when he publicly went to bat for Clinton. The unprecedented chest thumping pride, even mania Obama stirred among throngs of blacks was easy to understand. He was the Democrat that blacks desperately longed for and waited for him to come along and wipe away the horrid taste of the Bush years. He was a black man who they felt could actually win the big prize.

With the black vote firmly in hand, that gave him the freedom to craft his hope and change message in broad, bland, and especially non-racial terms. The idea was to avoid any appearance of a Jesse Jackson and Al Sharpton racial tilt. That would be the political kiss of death with many white voters.

That didn't change the political reality that black votes still provided the decisive edge for Obama in key primary state wins. Even in his losses to Hillary Clinton in Ohio, California and Texas in the February and March Democratic primaries, black votes kept the race close.

The myth that the black vote wins presidential election has been bandied about for so long that it has taken on the proportion of a political urban legend. In 2000, black voters made up nearly 11 percent of the overall voter. They gave the Democratic presidential contender Al Gore 90 percent of their vote. In 2004, black voters made up nearly 12 percent of the vote and gave Democratic presidential contender John Kerry 88 percent of the vote. Gore and Kerry lost.

The Clinton wins in 1992 and 1996 also helped fuel the myth that black votes put Democrats in the White House. Clinton managed to pry four Southern states out of the GOP orbit but he did it by downplaying racial and social issues and stressing family values, tough defense, and a strong economy. He got lots of white votes, especially, white male votes, and that made the difference since he got the same percentage of black votes that Democrats traditionally got in prior elections.

In 2004, then presidential contender Howard Dean openly worried that Democrats could not beat Bush unless they got a bigger share of white male votes. He quipped that the Democrats had to court beer-guzzling white guys who wave the Confederate flag. That brought howls of protests from Dean's Democratic rivals and the charge that Dean was pandering to unreconstructed bigots to get more white votes in his column. A livid Sharpton called Dean a turn coat Democrat and warned that heeding Dean would be a betrayal of black voters. They could have saved their breath. Kerry made only a weak, half-hearted effort to court white male voters in the South. Bush still got nearly seventy percent of the white male vote there, a second sweep of the South and a second term.

A chastised Dean got it right. He simply crunched the numbers and recognized that white males make up more than one-third of the electorate and their vote has been decisive in electing Republican presidents.

In 2000, exit polling showed that while white women backed Bush over Gore by 3 percentage points, white men backed him by 27 percentage points. Four years later the margin was 26 points for Bush over Kerry among white males.

The mix of euphoria and slavish devotion from blacks obviously was a major boost to Obama, but it had to be approached with extreme caution. In every election back to Lyndon Baines Johnson's smash victory over Barry Goldwater in 1964, blacks have been the most loyal foot soldiers for the Democrats. They gave every Democratic presidential candidate a ritual 80 to 90 percent of their vote. Even in the losing campaigns of Democratic presidential contenders against Ronald Reagan in 1980 and 1984, and George Bush Sr. in 1988, the top heavy black vote kept the election from being a total electoral blowout for Reagan and Bush Sr. But their votes didn't put candidates in the White House. The votes of white males, especially blue collar white males, did.

They posed the great threat to Obama's chances in the must win swing states of Pennsylvania and Ohio, as well as red state Indiana, and North Carolina. Even before the controversy over Jeremiah Wright in March, 2008 broke and Obama's perceived demeaning quip about blue collar whites and their penchant for guns and religion soured many of them toward him, he hadn't made much headway in bumping up his numbers among them.

A large percentage of these white male voters are conservative Democrats and independents. They liked Clinton's quasi populist economic message and were her trump card in the Democratic primaries. In exit polls, many of them minced no words and said that race did matter. That translated out to one quarter of Clinton backers who said that if Obama were the nominee they'd vote for McCain or turn into Election Day no-shows. At that point in the campaign it was simply talk and bluster. There was no real way to tell how many or how few of them really would cross party lines and vote for Mc-

Cain, or stay home. The likelihood was that Democratic Party loyalty along with the threat and fear of a personal economic belt tightening would make sure this was nothing more than an idle threat. The election subsequently showed it was mostly empty talk. Yet, in March, 2008 who could be really sure?

Obama was then caught in a Catch-22 dilemma. On the one hand he could not have come as far and as fast he did without the rock solid support of African-American voters. They gave him the big margins of victories in the South. On the other hand, he'd shown no ability to bridge the Bubba Gap.

The hard reality was that Obama couldn't win without black votes, and he couldn't win exclusively with them. It was a Catch-22. But fortunately it was one that was resolved in his favor by the two things that ultimately count most for a winning candidate—solid party loyalty and voter's sense that the economy works for or against their personal well-being in an election year. When it didn't, they kept party ranks in tact and punished the party they blamed for making things miserable for them. In 2008, that was Bush and the GOP.

CHAPTER 6

Oprah's Obama Nudge

I n mid-January, 2008 a throng of Oprah groupies pitched camp in front of the Obama campaign headquarters in Columbia, South Carolina to get free tickets to see her and Obama at the Colonial Center. They were there for the most part to ogle, and if they were lucky, touch the garments of America's favorite TV earth mother at the auditorium.

That didn't necessarily mean that they'd vote for Obama. A Pew Research Center poll after a big Oprah fundraising bash in September, 2007 found that, by a crushing margin, respondents said that Oprah's tout of Obama wouldn't sway them the least bit. Despite all the talk about Oprah being a transcendental force that supersedes mere celebrity mortals, she was still just that—a celebrity. The thousands that clawed for tickets to rub shoulders with Oprah at her Obama pep rally in Columbia were there precisely because of her star power and American's insatiable celebrity mania.

Celebrity endorsements, however, often fail miserably. Willie Nelson, Madonna, Jon Bovi, Martin Sheen and George Clooney are big-money celebrities and virtual household names. They all endorsed Democratic presidential candidates in 2004. Nelson endorsed Dennis Kucinich. Bon Jovi endorsed John Kerry. Sheen endorsed Howard Dean. Madonna backed Wesley Clark. One of their picks went down to flaming defeat. The other three never came close to getting the Democratic presidential nomination.

Clooney, meanwhile, publicly declared he hoped his non-endorsement of Kerry probably helped him at the polls. It didn't. Though Clooney backed Obama, he was still very mindful of the potential liability of fame and publicly said that he thought celebrity campaigning for a candidate hurt a candidate. Clooney recognized a political truism that's often etched in stone: A celebrity endorsement of a presidential candidate has little effect.

The hope was that the Oprah endorsement and push for black voter support for Obama might be different. The one group he hoped was the rare exception to this rule was black women. He banked on Oprah to help him smash through the Hillary love fest that many black women then had with the New York senator. In South Carolina, black voters made up nearly half of the Democratic voters—a greater proportion than any other state—and black women made up a significant proportion of that vote.

While most adored Oprah and were aware of her longstanding backing of Obama, at that early point in the campaign it didn't shake their support for Clinton. Nearly three times more black women said they'd back Hillary over him, and that was especially true among lower income, working-class black women. She was a woman, mother, and, most importantly, was regarded by many black women as a strong advocate for health care and women's interests.

Selling Obama was not like selling an author in Oprah's book club, where the mere mention of a name was a guarantee to send a book hurtling to the top of the charts. Voters make their decisions about politicians based on a combination of factors, party affiliation, and their stance on the issues, their political beliefs, and their experience in getting the job done. Few would rely on Oprah's word alone or her presence beside Obama to insure that he was the best person to handle global warming, tax policy, the Iraq war, terrorism, job creation, inflation, failing public schools, criminal justice issues or judicial appointments.

Only a candidate can forcefully and clearly articulate his or her grasp of the issues, and most importantly, convince voters that he or she is the most experienced. That was still Obama's exposed Achilles' heel at that time. In every poll, even the most rabid Clinton loathers ranked her at the top of the pile in experience in dealing with foreign and domestic issues. Voters got burned badly with Bush. His gross inexperience in statecraft before grabbing the White House cost Americans dearly as he bumbled and fumbled on everything from the Iraq war to domestic policy. Many voters didn't want to make that mistake again.

However, that doesn't mean the right endorsements wouldn't help a candidate. They had to be the right endorsements. Those endorsements come from seasoned politicians and respected industry, labor or public interest groups that have the trust and confidence of voters, and a solid track record in fighting for legislation and public policy change. That was not to say that Oprah's endorsement would not help Obama. The hype, promotion, and allure of Oprah would have value in raising his media visibility even higher. As it turned out that's exactly what her endorsement did for him.

The O and O show caused tongues to wag and eyebrows to rise. Oprah and Obama drew legions to their campaign stops. But more importantly, it marked another turning point for him. It helped him replace Hillary in the eyes and minds of many black voters as the candidate that they could back. In that instant, Oprah, the celebrity endorser, became Oprah the bonafide candidate deal maker.

CHAPTER 7

The Bradley Non-Effect

I n a speech on February 10, 2007 on the steps of the Old Capital Building in Springfield, Illinois, then first term U.S. Senator Barack Obama quashed months of doubts, speculation, and rumors. He formally announced that he was running for president. The announcement touched off obsessive chatter over whether race would ultimately derail Obama.

Obama made sure it didn't. In his 25 minute presidential candidacy announcement he used the word "race" exactly one time. And he did not use it as a direct racial reference. He used the word to make the point people could come together across all lines for change. The rest of the speech touched on ending the war, affordable health care, economic uplift and energy independence. These became the stock themes of his stump speeches. Obama did his political homework well.

He correctly gauged that many white Americans still harbor

racial biases and views about African-Americans. Polls during the campaign showed many whites, even those who passionately backed him, still clung tightly to the same old shop worn negative stereo- types about blacks.

That again raised the issue that the supposed Bradley Effect could be the Election Day spoiler. Some analysts warned the Brad- ley effect could account for 6 percentage points against an African- American candidate.

The Bradley Effect was the label that was slapped onto the al- leged penchant of many white voters to shade, deceive or just plain lie to pollsters and interviewers when they tell them color doesn't mean anything to them in an election. The Bradley Effect suppos- edly wrecked then Los Angeles Mayor Tom Bradley's bid to be the first black governor of California in 1986 when he ran against a white Republican candidate. Some polls had Bradley weeks before the elec- tion winning comfortably. The polls were faulty, fluid, and did not reflect other factors apart from race that hurt Bradley in the closing days of the campaign. Obama never publicly made mention of the Bradley Effect during the campaign. Though it did not really explain Bradley's loss, the possible misrepresenation by white voters of their true racial sentiments did cause Doug Wilder to sweat nervously on election night in Virginia before he squeaked out a win there for gov- ernor in 1989. It was also a possible factor in Harvey Gantt and Har- old Ford, Jr.'s losses in their Senate campaigns in North Carolina and Tennessee.

The Bradley Effect was murky, amorphous, and virtually defied fingering to the extent that it existed at all. Yet, when it came to judg- ing the worth of a candidate, race was only one often fuzzy factor voters considered in making a decision. The other compelling factors included their political loyalties, education, income, gender, sense of economic well-being or hardship, good feeling or foreboding about the future and the direction of the country. There were still more compelling factors such as a voter's personal convictions, religious beliefs, and visceral likes and dislikes. In some ways race recent elections began to slip in relevance and importance to big segments of voters.

In the last two decades, significant numbers of whites have voted for black candidates in senate, congressional, state legislative, gubernatorial, mayor, and city council races, even voting for them when their opponents were white. Obama was a textbook example of that. He was elected to the Illinois house, senate, and the U.S. Senate with top heavy white support.

Obama did more political homework and looked at what worked and didn't work for previous Democratic presidential contenders Al Sharpton and Jesse Jackson. They had three glaring liabilities. They were widely perceived as mostly protest candidates. They appealed almost exclusively to black voters. And they were also old line civil rights leaders. That stirred fear, even hostility, among many whites. If Obama had given even the slightest hint of a racial tilt in his campaign, his candidacy would have been dead at the starting gate. Obama prepped the political ground so well that he sold millions on the idea that he was not Jackson or Sharpton and that his campaign was solely about the issues that mattered to the broadest segment of Americans.

That paid huge dividends later when he faced the potential campaign killing crisis over his tie with his former pastor Jeremiah Wright.

His anguished, bare-the-soul speech in Philadelphia in March, 2008 that Wright did not speak for him, and that he was appalled to hear Wright's pulpit race thumping sermons was a tour de force. His supporters and even detractors accepted his explanation and refused to believe that he and Wright could have anything in common. The media which could have dug deep and probed into Obama's twenty year connection to Wright and inflicted a big wound on his campaign bought his explanation of racial innocence and dropped the matter.

There was also much talk inside and outside McCain's campaign and Republican circles about snatching at Obama's racial jugular and pounding him on his Wright connection. Other than a mild, tepid, half-hearted occasional mention of Wright, McCain largely steered clear of the controversy and the issue. When VP running mate Sarah Palin took a shot at Wright-Obama, McCain scotched any effort to beat up on the issue again. That, of course, didn't stop the GOP independent (hit) committees from hammering away with their last gasp saturation ads trying to smear Obama with Wright. But, the smear didn't take and there was no evidence that McCain or the Republican National Committee winked and nodded at the cheap shot attacks. Not that it would have mattered, the attacks changed absolutely nothing. If anything they probably angered many voters and made them quicken their steps to the polls to back Obama.

The Bradley Effect gave writers much to speculate about, pollsters to recalibrate their methods to take great care to safeguard that it wasn't a factor in their opinion samples, and Obama strategists to keep a hawk like watch in case it did actually become a factor. In the end it proved to be a myth, Team Obama and the voters made the Bradley Effect a non-effect.

CHAPTER 8

Jesse's Obama Hit Was a Blessing in Disguise

The fur flew between Jesse Jackson and Democratic presidential candidate Barack Obama after Jackson's alleged quip at a conference in France in October 2008 that an Obama White House would no longer put Israel's interests first. The alleged quip set off furious denials from Obama, loud protests from Jackson that he was misquoted, and screams of horror from legions of Obama backers that Jesse was again trying to sabotage Obama's campaign. The word "again," because Jesse was roundly condemned in July, 2008 when he was caught making a disparaging racial crack about Obama on an open mic duriing during a taping of a Fox Network news show.

But Jesse's Israel quip was time worn Jackson. He has repeatedly and unabashedly blasted the U.S.'s one sided tilt toward Israel over the years and has demanded a fair, balanced, and even handed policy toward the Palestinians. This position could hardly be called an extremist position, since former Democratic Presidents Carter, Clinton, and a parade of top domestic and foreign policy makers have said pretty much the same thing. Even Bush on past occasions has mildly rebuked Israel for its pulverizing attacks and assassinations of Palestinian leaders.

Yet it was only news when Jackson tied anything he said during the campaign into Obama, because, well, it was Jackson, and the inference was that anything Jackson said could hurt Obama. Nothing could have been further from the truth. In fact, it may have actually helped him.

Jackson is simply not the Jackson of a decade ago or even four years ago. That Jackson could instantly heat up a crowd with a timely slogan, catchy rhyme, or well-timed phrase and he had the instant ear of presidents and heads of state. However, the taint of sexual scandal and his fade from the headlines has wiped much of the luster off of his racial star.

Jackson belongs to the older civil rights generation, and he's found it tough-sledding trying to sell his civil rights pitch to upwardly mobile, younger blacks who have little inkling of past civil rights struggles. Jackson hinted at that in a brief speech in March, 2007 endorsing Obama when he said that it was time to pass the torch to a new generation of black politicians. This was self-serving and disingenuous.

Jackson never had any intention of passing that torch on to anyone, least of all Obama. Since Obama's rocket launch Jackson continued to do everything he could to micromanage a role for himself on the national political scene. But even if Jackson had been a rock solid Obama man, and still had the sheen on his leadership badge, he was a totally different political type than Obama.

Obama is a moderate centrist Democrat who bagged the White House by being everything that Jackson isn't. Despite his fall from leadership grace, Jesse is still widely and indelibly typed as a polarizing, race baiter.

However, that didn't mean that Jesse was irrelevant, or even that he couldn't give some aid to Obama. Obama still needed a massive turnout of black voters in the three absolute must win states of Ohio, Florida, and Pennsylvania to seal a White House win. The overwhelming majority of black voters there would vote for him. But they also had to turn out in record numbers. Jackson could help make that happen. And though Obama would never dare publicly seek his help to insure a record turnout, Obama operatives tacitly and quietly encouraged Jackson to rev up the (black) crowds and boost the voter numbers.

But Jackson was really manna from heaven for Obama in another way. By criticizing him, his Fox TV racial remark, his invisible presence in any capacity in the Obama campaign, his anti-Israel tag on Obama and his vehement denunciation of it, in a back hand way further burnished Obama's credentials as a race neutral and all purpose moderate Democrat. A Democrat who was not beholden to and would not be a captive of the old guard race-is-everything civil rights leaders.

Obama's candidacy would never have gotten off the launch pad if there was even the slightest inkling of any allegiance to Jackson and the thinking of Jackson. In the closing days of the campaign the obsessive question that continued to be on the lips of many was, would enough centrist and undecided white voters do what most of them profusely professed publicly, and that was to punch the ticket for a qualified African-American presidential candidate?

A too out front Jackson in tow with Obama would have insured that most wouldn't do that. But Jackson carping at Obama , whether real or simply manufactured, was the added insurance Obama needed to ensure many white independent voters would punch his ticket. Many ultimately did, and Jackson's hit and then invisibility in the campaign was a blessing in disguise for Obama.

CHAPTER 9

The Reverend Wright Question Mark

"There were early warning signals of the ugliness that could come... the message was that Obama was not exempt from a racial dig. That was also evident in the knock at Obama's Southside Chicago church, or to be more exact the minister at the church, Jeremiah Wright. He is an outspoken afro-centric activist on racial and social issues. The inference was that Obama's guilt by membership and friendship with him made him a closet radical and a race baiter."

This writer wrote these words in a column January 6, 2008. That was two months before the Obama-Wright connection flap hit the airwaves. It was a no-brainer prediction that the Wright card would eventually be played hard by the GOP and some in the media who milked for all it was worth. The inflammatory, provocative speeches of Wright were well-known. Thousands within and without his church had heard them for years. His afro-centric tinged writings were widely cited by black commentators. It was only a matter of time.

The only surprise was the timing. This writer expected the Wright card would be kept tightly in the political deck and dumped on the political table by the GOP "truth squads" in the late days of the campaign if Obama were the eventual Democratic presidential nominee. But then again, why not dump it on the table sooner if it could damage him. The Wright quips were just too juicy, racially salacious, and media sensational to keep under wraps any longer. If Obama could be hammered with and tainted by the guilt by association tag with Wright that would further poison the Democratic Party well and make the pack of independents who were beginning to lean to Obama waver, maybe even rethink just who and what they were getting into by backing him.

This writer didn't just make the prediction that the Wright card would sooner or later be used against Obama. He also flatly predicted the instant Obama stood on the steps of the Old Capitol building in Springfield, Illinois in February 2007 and announced he was on a history making quest to be president, that two things would happen. The first was that the racial innuendos, rumors, gossip, hints, digs, and finger-pointing would be a subtle and at least some in the GOP hoped a damaging subtext to his campaign.

The second thing was that he couldn't totally duck and dodge racial matters by simply pounding away that he and his campaign was about hope, change and unity. That was good campaign stump stuff but it was not the reality of race and politics in America.

His race speech in Philadelphia in March, 2008 was the obvious answer, in fact the only answer to head off trouble. Obama did the obligatory sprint backwards from Wright's preachments and philosophy. The idea was not just to distance himself from Wright's views, but to get ahead of the curve and reassure the doubters about him that his hope, change and unity theme was still alive and well.

The pressure was on. He made the speech under extreme duress, namely the beating that he took for his association with Wright, and his fear that it could wreck or at the very least be a horrible distraction to his campaign. As he correctly noted, the Wright speech(s) would continue to resurface and would continue to be a prick in his campaign's side. But it also wouldn't open up any new dialogue on race that some commentators naively thought would or should happen. Obama in fact told us why that was true in the speech. He mentioned the O.J. Simpson case, and how the great racial discourse that the case supposedly ignited was grotesquely twisted, mangled, and ultimately botched.

That didn't mean race would magically disappear from the presidential campaign trail, or more specifically from Obama's campaign trail. Those questions would still be whispered or shouted out whenever Obama's name was mentioned: Was America ready for a black president? Would whites vote for him in a showdown with a white male? Did he really have the experience (read intelligence and competence)? Was he patriotic enough? Was he black enough? Was he too black? Would he tilt toward blacks and other minorities in the White House? Would he be a yes man for (white) corporate interests? Would his election make race a dead issue in America?

None of this made for serious dialogue on racial problems, let alone pointing America in the direction of real solutions to them. This was mere momentary racial titillation. Obama's speech contained the seed for the racial discourse opening when he spoke of the disparities in the criminal justice system, failing inner city schools, HIV/AIDS, chronic and nagging Great Depression high rate of black male unemployment, the need for greater family supports. But he was careful to speak of them only in the broadest of generalities. There was not the barest hint of any specific initiatives to tackle these problems. That would have only opened up the lid to ask more distracting even dangerous questions on race and society.

The Wright issue and by extension race, was forced on Obama. His eloquent speech didn't make them go away, but the speech had to be made to further insure that race if not exactly off the nation's table would at least be off Obama's campaign table. The media and much of the public saw, heard, agreed, and then moved on. Wright would surface again in an 11th Hour last gasp effort by the GOP front Trust Fund committee a couple of days before Election Day to taint Obama. The hit ads featured the same old fiery, inflammatory clip of Wright interspersed with shots of him and Obama embracing. Predictably, it flopped again. The Wright question mark had been answered in Obama's favor.

CHAPTER 10

How Obama Snatched the Race Card off the Presidential Table

A handful of top advisors in the McCain camp were perplexed at their boss's flat refusal to again slam Democratic rival Barack Obama on his ties to his former pastor Jeremiah Wright. Instead they picked the race neutral target of former Weather Underground terrorist Bill Ayers, and tried to tie Obama to him. That ploy had no public or media legs.

A GOP official explained that McCain did not dredge up the Wright-Obama connection because he did not want to be seen as a racist. That's probably true. But in a close to the wire election, a candidate will grab at any weapon to get an edge, and the GOP has never flinched at using race as a weapon when it suited its purpose. And indeed McCain's running mate Sarah Palin chomped at the bit to snatch at the Wright issue. But the word was hands off.

There are several reasons suggested why Palin and the GOP did not go for the racial jugular with Obama. One reason offered is that the GOP is smitten with racial guilt too. The idea that Obama benefits unduly from that was much talked about, and probably much overblown during the campaign.

Psychologists say guilt stems from a deep feeling on the part of an individual who committed a wrong through neglect, dislike, or injury to another. It manifests itself in anxiety, remorse, anguish, and depression. Obama was a candidate for president, not an innocent victim who someone splattered on the side of the road in an accident, or a child or relative who someone harmed and now felt an acute need for atonement. In that case the atonement would be to vote for Obama solely to make up for the decades of racial abuse heaped on blacks. That was a stretch.

Obama was hardly the first African-American politician who had gotten elected wholly or with substantial white votes. The list stretching back years from Los Angeles Mayor Tom Bradley to Massachusetts governor Deval Patrick is legion. Former Tennessee Congressman Harold Ford, Jr. in his run for the U.S. Senate is oft cited as a victim of white polling voting booth duplicity. Yet he still got more than 40 percent of the white vote in his election defeat.

McCain's decision not to make race an issue was not totally due to honor and noble intent. A too frontal racial attack would have brought instant screams of foul from Democrats, and millions of voters who demanded that the campaign be a clean, issues focused campaign. McCain read the political leaves correctly and saw the political peril in flipping the race card. The occasions that he slipped and rapped Obama as a socialist and a terrorist fellow traveler brought universal condemnation that he was going negative or worse running a dirty campaign.

Obama helped things even more. The firm message in his signature slogan of hope and change, on campaign literature, TV ads, rallies, in pitches to contributors, his core of advisors, and major endorsers was that the Obama presidential campaign and an Obama presidency would be broad, non-racial and issues driven. Anything else would have instantly stirred horrifying visions to many of Sharpton and Jackson. His candidacy would have been DOA.

But McCain and Obama's best efforts to make race a non issue in the campaign would have fallen short without the sea change shift in public attitudes. The decade from the mid-1990s on since the Rodney King beating, the O.J. Simpson trial, and the urban riots, was a period of relative racial peace in America. During that time polls consistently showed that more whites than ever before were genuinely convinced that America was a color-blind society, equal opportunity is a reality, and blacks and whites if not exactly attaining complete social and economic equality, were closer than ever to that goal. Though the figures on income, education and health care still show a colossal gap between poor blacks and whites, the perception nonetheless is that racism is an ugly and nasty byproduct of a long by-gone past.

The passage by huge margins of anti-affirmative action measures in California, Michigan, and Washington since the mid-1990s was not simply a case of whites engaging in racial denial or a cover for hidden bias. Many white voters backed the initiatives because they honestly believed color should never be in the equation in hiring and education, and that race is divisive.

It's easy to see why they believe that. "Whites only" signs and redneck Southern cops unleashing police dogs, turning fire hoses on and beating hapless black demonstrators have long been forgotten. Americans turn on their TVs and see legions of black newscasters and talk show hosts, topped by TV's richest and most popular celebrity, Oprah Winfrey.

They see mega-rich black entertainers and athletes pampered and fawned over by a doting media and an adoring public. They see TV commercials that picture blacks living in trendy integrated suburban homes, sending their kids to integrated schools and driving expensive cars. They see blacks such as former Secretary of State Colin Powell and his successor Condoleezza Rice in high-profile policy-making positions in the Bush administration. They see dozens of blacks in Congress, many more in state legislatures and city halls. They see blacks heading corporations and universities.

Obama's fresh face, new politics pitch for hope, change, and unity touched a nerve with whites, especially young whites. This had nothing to do with race, let alone any guilt over slavery or lynchings. These atrocities were simply too far removed in time and space from whites, especially young whites, for them to feel any need to do an Election Day mea culpa.

McCain went out of his way at one of his campaign rallies to tell a few loudmouths to knock off the race tinged bashing of Obama. That was the right thing to do. Once Palin got the word not to tar Obama with Wright again, she made no more mention his name. That was also the right thing to do. If McCain couldn't win the presidency by hitting Obama hard on the legitimate issues of the economy, the war, health care, taxes, and the Wall Street meltdown, then he didn't deserve to win. Race in that case wouldn't have helped him anyway

CHAPTER 11

Sí Se Puede

A day before the Puerto Rican primary election on June 1, 2008, I talked with several Mexican workers and business professionals during a visit to Mexico City. The subject was American presidential politics and the upcoming election. They had only the haziest notion that Obama was the frontrunner for the Democratic Party nomination. They knew virtually nothing about his positions on the major issues, especially the hot button issue of immigration reform. They all readily recognized Clinton's name and thought that if elected she'd do a better job on the immigration question.

Their haziness in not knowing that Obama was the odds on favorite to bag the Democratic presidential nomination and even their wariness toward him was not a surprise. Three of the top newspapers on the newsstands in Mexico City, *Excelsior, El Universal,* and *Reforma* made only bare mention of the Puerto Rican primary, and only passing mention of the aftermath.

That had to change for Obama. Latino voters now made up one in five Democratic voters. They could put the GOP strongholds in Texas, Nevada, Colorado and swing state Florida in play for the Democrats. But that was only if Obama could stoke the enthusiasm, passion and allegiance of Latino voters. In the early days of the campaign, Obama failed to light a fire under them. The explanation was an easy one. Hispanic voters simply didn't know who he was and what he stood for. That and their familiarity with, loyalty to, and even like of

Clinton by the majority of Latino voters at that stage of the Democratic primaries was a tormenting dilemma for him and the Democrats. Polls showed he would do well against McCain. That was mostly because a majority of Latino voters in Texas, California, New Jersey, and New York were Democrats. These are the states in which Latino voters helped propel Clinton to a decisive win over Obama in the primaries. In the contest against McCain, Obama's numbers still paled in comparison to what Clinton would do against him.

But even before Clinton's crushing win over Obama in Puerto Rico there were warning signs that Obama's Latino dilemma wouldn't go away. In Nevada in January, 2008 Obama got the endorsement of the leaders of the heavily Hispanic Culinary Workers Union. Yet getting the vote of the rank and file union workers was a far different matter, as the subsequent vote showed. Latino voters, many of them almost certainly members of the culinary union, defied their leaders and their votes made a big difference in Clinton's victory in the state.

Obama spent months on the campaign trail, got non-stop media exposure, the nod of big name Democrats, did a victory romp through a dozen primary states, and piled up a commanding number of delegates. That slowly began to turn the tide. By April 2008, polls clearly showed that a majority of Latino voters had warmed up to him. The later endorsement of one time Democratic presidential contender Bill Richardson and a legion of leading Hispanic union leaders, elected officials, and top Latino entertainers pushed Obama's polling numbers among Hispanics up higher.

A May, 2008 poll in California showed Obama would beat McCain handily and that he would get more than sixty percent of the Latino vote. In the election he got nearly seventy percent of the Hispanic vote in the state. This was not a small campaign footnote. Latino voters make up about one quarter of California voters. Their swelling numbers were almost certainly a major reason why even though McCain publicly announced he would not write California off even though a GOP presidential contender hadn't won the state since George Bush Sr. in 1988, there was absolutely no chance Mc-Cain would get close to the forty percent Latino vote support that W. Bush got. The GOP's immigration hostile stance in Congress and among top GOP leaders, exclusive of McCain, alienated huge numbers of Latinos, even those Latinos who backed Bush in 2004. With Clinton out of the race in June, 2008 and actively campaigning for Obama, and with every major Latino national organization pledging to work hard on his behalf, his Latino vote numbers began to surge higher still.

Obama's heightened name identification, media boost, energizing change pitch and personal charisma worked wonders in helping to dispel the mix of wariness, indifference, and outright opposition to him that I heard from Mexican workers and professionals in Mexico City. On Election Day Obama did what Kerry or Gore couldn't do.

He got nearly sixty percent of Florida's Hispanic vote. Nationally, he won sixty-six percent of the Hispanic vote. Obama made si se puede more than just a throw away Spanish thumping campaign slogan for him and the Democrats. He made it a reality.

CHAPTER 12

Obama: The Racial Exception?

A n odd, even bizarre thing happened soon after Obama tossed his hat in the presidential rink in February 2007. A hodgepodge of avowedly racist groups burned up internet sites not with rage, but glee. They were giddy at the thought that Obama might win.

Their rationale was that an African-American in the White House would prove their point that blacks were out to dominate whites and that whites would be so disgusted that they would unite in righteous and very racist anger. This in turn would trigger their long swooned over racist fantasy of a race war. This was dismissed for what it was, namely the rantings of the racist lunatic fringe. But that didn't mean many whites who harbor hidden or even conscious racial animus against blacks wouldn't back Obama albeit for their own reasons.

A mid-September, 2008 survey found that about one quarter of whites held negative views of blacks that were top heavy with the old shop worn stereotypes. The respondents said blacks used race as a crutch, were not as industrious as whites, opposed interracial marriage, and were terrified of black crime (Obama mildly chided his white grandmother in his so-called race speech in March, 2008 for saying she feared black men). Yet nearly a quarter of them claimed that they'd vote for Obama. They were as good as their word. Obama got more than forty percent of the white vote, a higher percentage than either Democratic presidential contenders Al Gore and John Kerry got in their election bids in 2000 and 2004.

The standard explanation for this seeming racial schizoid view was that many conservative whites were so hammered by financial hardship that the economy trumped race and that Obama would do more to help them out of their financial hole than McCain. Others liked him because his race neutral campaign was a soothing departure from the perceived race baiting antics of Jesse Jackson and Al Sharpton. Still others liked him because his racially exotic background supposedly didn't fit that of the typical African American.

There was truth in these reasons cited to explain Obama's appeal to some racial bigots. But there's another reason that wasn't cited. That was the long, checkered, and tortured history of racial exceptionalism. That's the penchant for some whites to make artificial distinctions between supposedly good and bad blacks. That's apparent in the unthinking, offensive, insulting, and just plain dumb crack made to some articulate, well-educated blacks in business and the professions that they are "different than other blacks or not like other blacks."

Racial exceptionalism also stems from the ingrained, but terribly misplaced, belief that blacks are perennially disgruntled, hostile, and rebellious, and are always on the lookout for any real or perceived racial slight, and itch to pick a fight over it. An African-American who doesn't fit that type is touted, praised, even anointed by some as the reasoned voice of black America.

A century ago the mantle of the reasoned, exceptional African-American was bestowed on famed educator, Booker T. Washington. He was showered with foundation and corporate largesse. In the 1920s and 30s, NAACP leaders always found a ready welcome at the White House. They were praised in the press and bankrolled by some industrialists. In the 1960s, Urban League President Whitney Young, NAACP executive secretary Roy Wilkins, and Martin Luther King Jr. before he fell out of favor with the Lyndon Johnson White House after his too vocal opposition to the Vietnam War and turn to economic radicalism, were lionized for their reason and racial moderation.

In the 1980s, Presidents Reagan and Bush Sr. actively cultivated and promoted a bevy of younger GOP friendly black academics, business leaders, and conservatives. Reagan and Bush Sr. plainly saw them as a leadership alternative to the black Democrats and the old guard civil rights leaders. The black conservatives were appointed to government posts, bagged foundation grants, were feted by conservative think tanks, and their columns were routinely published in major newspapers. They were continually cited by writers and reporters as a breath of fresh air among African-Americans mostly for their willingness to break ranks with and to blister Jackson, Sharpton, and the civil rights establishment.

Obama hardly fit the mold of a black conservative, but neither was he the ultra-liberal Democrat that some conservative opponents routinely painted him as. Even before his rocket launch to the threshold of the presidency, he was considered a moderate, centrist Democrat, a consummate party insider, and a rising Beltway establishment politician. Without that stamp of mainstream approval, his White House bid would have never gotten to political first base.

Obama bristled publicly at the notion that he was in competition with or a critic of civil rights leaders, or that he was immune from racial jabs. He repeatedly praised past civil rights leaders for their heroic battle against racial injustice. That was good, but that didn't erase the nagging habit to elevate some blacks above the racial fray, and declare them the exception. That included those white bigots who said they'd back Obama.

Book 3
Power, Politics
and the Campaign

CHAPTER 13

Exorcising the GOP's Obama Demon

In June, 2008, former Republican Presidential candidate Mike Huckabee sternly warned the GOP that demonizing Barack Obama wouldn't work and it would be a big blunder to even try. Huckabee issued the warning because he was worried that in going negative against Obama the GOP risked voter backlash. McCain agreed. He repeatedly pledged that his campaign would be clean.

McCain's clean campaign vow and Huckabee's warning against going negative didn't mean much too some GOP-connected 527 independent expenditure committees (uncharitably branded hit squads). Under an IRS loophole independent expenditure committees can get funds from any source with no limit. They could spend the money pretty much anyway they wanted. The instant it became clear that Obama would likely get the Democratic nod a few independent committees swung into action.

They ran campaign ads in a couple of primary states knocking him for ties to his controversial former pastor Jeremiah Wright and questioned his patriotism. The committees hoped to spend a mini-Fort Knox storehouse of privately funneled dollars to slam Obama on any and every big, petty, and almost always personal attack, issue they chose. Other than publicly disavowing any of the digs that hit Obama below the belt, McCain couldn't do anything about them.

The question, though, was whether demonizing a candidate really worked? The two best known examples are the Willie Horton hit against Democratic presidential contender Michael Dukakis in 1988 and the Swift Boat blindside of Democratic presidential contender John Kerry in 2004. One stoked the fears of crime (Dukakis). The other planted doubts about character (Kerry). In both instances, they worked.

Even without these extreme cases, there's evidence that going negative can work. Though surveys showed that the overwhelming majority of voters abhor personal smears against candidates and are turned off by them, far too many voters also can be influenced by the negative stuff they hear about a candidate. The trick to implant the negative belief is that the ads must be directly linked to the candidate's political position on the issues, style or even personality. In April, 2008 the GOP-connected Legacy Committee loudly announced that it planned to hammer Obama as being soft on crime in attack ads in several states.

The committee tied this softer version of the Horton attack on him directly to his vote in the Illinois state legislature against expanding the death penalty for gang related murders. The law was superfluous and political pandering since there were already tough laws on the books that proscribed the death penalty for these types of atrocious crimes. Obama publicly stated his support of the death penalty for certain "heinous" crimes including gang related murders.

Yet, Obama's vote, and the fact that he was tarred as a liberal Democrat, gave the hit committee just enough of a hook to hinge their ad on and hope the soft on crime tag would stick. It was virtually assured that the committees would dredge up some of the old stuff about Wright, Obama's youthful self-admitted drug use, and financial dealings with convicted Chicago financier Tony Rezko, his wafer thin connection with former Weather Underground terrorist Bill Ayers, and some outdated remarks he made about the Middle East and economic fairness in the mid-1990s. That would be twisted into his being a closet terrorist and socialist.

The more highbrow committees would continue to work him over as being too liberal and too soft on national security concerns (with more subtle digs at his patriotism). Then there was the inexperience label that Obama was saddled with from the start of his campaign. That would be tossed out repeatedly with the hope that it would imprint him as a greenhorn who would bumble and stumble on policy issues if entrusted with the highest office; in other words a Democratic version of Bush.

The one potential hit issue that the committees knew to tread gingerly on was race. It was widely thought to have derailed a few black candidates in past elections that were considered shoo-in winners in head to head contests with white opponents. Race was brought up to tie Obama to Wright, but it wouldn't be used as a major attack weapon against him. It was simply too sensitive and risky a ploy and would likely backfire anyway.

Huckabee's admonition to the GOP shadow groups not to go negative fell on deaf ears. But they fell flat on their face for two reasons. One, the committees simply didn't have cash in 2008 that they had in year's past, and there was the fear of being fined for straying to far over the line of what was permissible to say and spend. After the 2004 election some of the 527s were indeed slapped with hefty fines. The second more compelling reason is that the majority of voters were more concerned about their pocketbooks than someone had been at a party with Ayers a decade earlier, smoked a joint as a youngster, or sat in Wright's church at one time.

Though Obama couldn't out McCain McCain on the GOP's trump cards of national security and terrorism, again if it was a matter of who could do the better job on the economy, jobs, affordable health care, a war wind down, voters again consistently said the Democrats would do it better than the GOP. That issue was and remained Obama's trump cards as it was for every Democratic president or presidential candidate dating back to Democrat, Harry Truman in 1948 who first beat back the GOP's smear of being too liberal, radical, and any other demon that a Democrat could be bedeviled with.

Obama proved that was one demon that could be exorcised.

CHAPTER 14

The Clinton Factor

The clamor for an Obama-Clinton dream ticket started virtually the moment they started their head to head slog through the primaries and the caucuses from January through June, 2008. Top Democrats really wanted Clinton to do a full court campaign press for Obama. The idea was that Clinton as an Obama campaigner would be able to sway the millions of wavering, disgruntled, and even hostile Democrats to Obama.

However, the clamor for her as Obama's VP was absurd. The notion that she could cajole doubting Democrats to change their mind about Obama was shaky at best. First there was the notion of Clinton as VP. Obama effectively killed that when he appointed a Clinton-unfriendly committee to search out a VP pick. And it was just as well he did. A major McCain attack point against Obama was that he was a much too liberal Democrat, and an elitist, who was way out of touch with moderate-to-conservative mainstream America. Putting another liberal Democrat and a woman at that on the ticket, especially one with the towering negatives that Clinton had among ultraconservatives and Christian fundamentalists would have been the ultimate political gift from heaven to McCain.

McCain's other prime attack point was that he was the toughest, most experienced, and most knowledgeable on national security, the war on terrorism, and defense preparedness. Clinton would have done absolutely nothing to help Obama neutralize that knock against him. But what about Clinton as a full throttle campaigner who could win over the doubting Obama Hillary Democrats? They were the blue collar, rural, older, non-college educated whites, and a large block of Latino voters. She didn't have much value there either. The Latino voters that backed Clinton were solid Democrats anyway and would have voted for whoever won the eventual Democratic presidential nomination.

As for blue collar whites, especially white males, the hard truth was that many did not vote for her because they liked her and her policies, they didn't like Obama, and she was the only other Democrat on the ticket. The reasons they didn't like him—racial fear, distrust, uncertainty, his inexperience, patriotism questions, and a too liberal voting record—weren't going to instantly vanish just because Clinton told them they should vote for him. That would require changing political circumstances, an economic sea change, i.e. a collapsing economy, a massive Obama and Democratic Party campaign organizational effort, and a little luck.

The other sobering political reality Obama had to face about Clinton was that millions of voters backed her in the primaries, but millions more rejected her, and these were mostly Democratic voters. Her negatives, and she had more than any other Democratic or Republican candidate, didn't vanish in the primaries. She was a Clinton, was viewed as the consummate old school Washington insider, stirred visceral loathing among ultra conservatives, and was a liberal.

Polls consistently showed far more voters said they'd vote for an African-American for president before a woman. The shock of a woman and an African-American on the Democratic ticket, and a woman named Clinton at that, would do something McCain only had tepid success in doing.That was to inflame Christian fundamentalist and ultraconservatives to storm the polls to back him.

Even if Clinton was not a Clinton, and a woman, she would upset the very thing that every presidential nominee must have on their ticket, and that's chemistry and balance. She would upset both for Obama in two ways. She, as Obama, is a liberal Democrat from a big Northern state. This would've jeopardized the chance Obama had of pulling one or two of the Southern and heartland states out of the iron grip the GOP has had on them for a quarter century. The legions of non-college educated, rural and blue collar Democrats who found Obama politically (and racially) unpalatable would find him no more palatable with Clinton at his side. The GOP independent committees would've endlessly looped Clinton primary hammer blows at Obama as being elitist and out of touch with "hard working, white Americans."

Those loops would've made both Obama and Clinton look silly paired together. Both would've had to spent endless time trying to refute her old attack statements against him. She would have further upended the chemistry and balance by forcing Obama to spend just as much time assuring voters that he, not Clinton (and Bill), would be making and implementing vital policy decisions.

Obama never gave the slightest public hint that he was interested in teaming with Clinton. Clinton never gave any public hint that she was remotely interested in playing second fiddle to him.

Clinton was a loyal Democratic team player and while she would not have been the asset many thought that she would be as a VP on the Obama ticket, she did have important stump value on the campaign trail, and even more importantly as the final piece in the Obama push for the absolutely critical Democratic Party unity against McCain.

Clinton assured that value and support with her rousing speech at the Democratic convention in which she pumped him and his candidacy and savaged Bush and McCain's policies. That sent the right and needed signal that the Clintons were finally firmly on board the Obama train. That further ensured that the Clinton factor would be a real factor not a liability in Obama's White House push

CHAPTER 15

Shoring Up the Vice Presidential Flank

The rule of thumb in picking vice presidents is that they must do three things. They must balance the ticket, make up for a real or perceived deficit the presidential contender has, and hopefully help him win the presidency, or at the very least don't help him lose it. That rule of vice presidential thumb applied more than ever to Obama and McCain.

The balance part was easy to handicap for Obama. His pick, first of all had to be a he. The talk about Hillary Clinton was just that talk. She is a Northern, moderate Democrat, as is Obama. She is a woman with lots of personal and political baggage. She would've piled the X

Factor of gender bias to what was for a time the worrisome X Factor of racial bias on top of Obama.

He must be an older, centrist to conservative Democrat from the South or the Midwest. The names that at first were bandied about Tim Kaine, Evan Bayh, and Sam Nunn pretty much fit that bill. Bill Clinton was the one recent exception who defied the rule of thumb on balance in picking a VP. Al Gore, like him, was a young, Southern Baptist. It worked because Clinton needed Gore to bolster his pitch that he was not another stereotypical tax and spend, soft on crime, weak on military and national security Democrat. This was the traditional attack point that every Republican going back to Richard Nixon in 1968 hammered their Democratic opponent on.

Obama needed a VP who would be the walking, talking, and voting candidate to foil McCain's biggest attack point against him and that was his razor thin to non-existent credential as a tough guy on national security. A Pew Research Center poll in June, 2008 found that nearly half of Americans still said Obama was not tough enough on national security and McCain was. Most voters still ranked the economy as their number one worry, and that supposedly worked to Obama's favor. But national security was still a troubling enough issue for Obama to protect his flank on.

The other McCain hammer point was Obama's relative inexperience. The irony is that Bush got the same knock. He did the smart thing, and shut down that avenue of attack when he picked Dick Cheney. Cheney was older, had been in and out of several GOP administrations, and was the consummate party insider.

Obama's vice presidential pick was a high stakes game.

The selection of the VP in the 2008 presidential election year was more than just a standard dressing up of the presidential ticket. He had to be able to actually help Obama win. There have been a few times in past elections when VPs have made a difference. Lyndon Johnson in 1960 was the textbook example of that. He brought legislative savvy, he was a Southern then still in good stead with the white South, and he could deliver two or three Deep South states. He did his job. Bush Sr. also helped Reagan in 1980. He brought experience, insider connections, and as a transplanted Southerner, the regional balance that Reagan needed. And he was moderate enough to give Reagan a little edge with moderate Republicans.

If Obama had been able to widen the poll gap comfortably over McCain before the last two months of the campaign, the vice presidency would still have been important, but not as crucial. That didn't happened. So the VP had to do something that seldom happens, he had to shore up Obama's flank.

Enter Joe Biden. His long years on the Senate Foreign Relations Committee put him at the center of action and even decision making on key foreign policy matters. His centrist stance on the war, plus his age, he was 65, and elder statesman image made him the made-in-heaven choice.

Obama was hardly the first recent presidential candidate deemed a neophyte, if not hopelessly far behind on the learning curve, on foreign policy and national security issues. W. Bush carried the same political albatross. He did the smart political thing and picked the older, experienced two stints Secretary of Defense Dick Cheney as his running mate. He reassured party regulars that the White House would not stumble when hit with a foreign policy crisis. It did on Iraq, but at the time the perception was that it was the right move.

McCain's attacks weren't the only things Obama heeded in picking Joe. Obama took heed of history. President Bush in 2004 pounded Democratic rival John Kerry in 2004 as being soft of anti-terrorism and national security. Kerry didn't get it. He picked moderate Southern Democrat, John Edwards, as his running mate. It didn't do a thing to help Kerry burnish his credentials as strong on Bush's signature issues. In 2008, they weren't the compelling issues that scared and concern millions of voters as they did in 2004. Yet they were still issues that resonated with millions of voters, especially the much coveted, moderate to conservative independent voters.

Finally, Obama heeded the polls. Republicans and independents said they wanted a VP who had solid national security and foreign policy credentials. Democrats said the same thing. In a July, 2008 poll by the Clarus Research Group, a majority of Democrats rated foreign policy and national security just below the economy as key concerns, and that the Democratic VP should have strong credentials on both.

A massive viral email stealth campaign had kicked into high gear on the internet targeting Obama on his national security toughness. It didn't stop there. This slippery campaign also questioned his patriotism. Before the West Virginia primary in May, 2008, a piqued Obama snapped at one reporter who questioned whether white voters in the state saw him as un-American even though he was a practicing Christian and his grandfather was a World War II vet.

Biden was on the ticket mostly to counter McCain's hit point that Obama was a greenhorn on foreign policy and national security. It did. It shored up Obama's alleged anemic credentials on foreign policy and national security. In this case, the VP did not hurt but helped Obama's election.

CHAPTER 16

The Palin Gamble

It was a foregone conclusion among many observers that if McCain lost two things would do him in. One of them he couldn't control. That was the economy, not its collapse, but when it collapsed. In a look at how six of eight presidents fared since 1948 when the economy went on the rocks or appeared to go on the rocks, three were beaten and three beat back their challengers. If the economy went bad toward the end of a president's term, voters were much more likely to blame and punish not just the president but also his party.

McCain was not Bush as he pointedly reminded Obama in their last televised debate in October, 2008. But he was the GOP presidential standard bearer, and he had to take the heat for the GOP's real and perceived economic sins. That hurt and hurt bad. McCain's slogans and shouts about country first, along with his subtle and open knocks at Bush and the GOP couldn't change that.

He could do something about his vice-presidential pick and Mc-
Cain was if anything a good listener. The instant he heard the loud
squeals from Republican pro-life hawks that his campaign would
be DOA if he dared tried to shove former Homeland Security Chief
Tom Ridge or maverick Senator Joe Lieberman on the ticket, he back
pedaled fast. Both are moderates on abortion. And that made them
anathema to the hawks.

We'll never know whether McCain's brief float of their names
as GOP VP possibilities was a trial balloon, a deft feint, or just loose
talk. But it did set things up nicely for Alaska Governor Sarah Palin.
Despite much talk from McCain's camp and the pro and con pundit
chatter touting her as being fresh, young, a reformer, anti-GOP establishment and an ingenious pick, or slamming her as a political school
girl novice, and a disastrous pick, the fact was that Palin was on the
ticket to assuage the pro-life hawks. But more importantly, she was
there to fire up the millions of men and women voters who demand
that a GOP presidential candidate firmly oppose abortion. That's the
price for their vote.

He also gambled that she could bag a big swatch of disgruntled
Hillary Democratic women, rev up the Christian fundamentalists,
and burnish his claim to be the Washington outsider. The hope was
that social conservatives would flood the polls on Election Day. The
problem was that Palin, as events amply showed, was a social conservative with a mini-telephone book of negatives who at times turned
out to be SNL laughingstock fodder. What she gave to the ticket she
also took away.

Worse she also put an issue back on the table, Obama's table that
is, that McCain had struggled mightily to take off namely his age and

health. A big percentage of voters still said they had huge reservations about McCain, because of his age. This fear led back to Palin. There was stark horror among untold numbers of voters at the thought of having her only a heartbeat away from the presidency.

The Palin pick was the biggest single reason why long time rock solid GOP Party regulars and a slew of Reagan and W. Bush and Bush Sr. appointees did the unprecedented. They jumped ship to back Obama.

However, what about the abortion issue? Could Palin have really helped McCain on this? Several major polls since 2003 have shown that while the abortion question at times slid lower on the public's issue radar scope, it never has slipped entirely off it. Americans have been almost evenly divided between those who call themselves pro-choice and pro-life. In the five presidential elections between 1984 and 2000 the majority of voters who said abortion was a major issue for them, backed the GOP candidate. Pro-life leaning voters were more likely to dash to the polls to back the GOP candidate.

A Gallup Values and Belief survey in May, 2008 measured the effect of pro and anti-abortion sentiment on the presidential race. It found the pro life voter edge translated out to about a 2 to 3 percent bump up for the GOP presidential candidate.

In a runaway election for either the Democratic or GOP presidential candidate that percent wouldn't mean much. In a tight down to the wire election that percentage jump could be huge.

The dilemma for Obama was how to defuse the pro-life hot box. The obvious counter was to fire up pro choice advocates. They also number in the millions, and an aroused, impassioned plea to them and their march to the polls potentially could give Obama the bump up he needed from the pro choice side. NARAL-Pro Choice America and NOW wasted no time in lambasting McCain and Palin. They called his picking her a cynical ploy and smoking gun proof that he was a rigid extremist on abortion. The blasts were timely, hard hitting, and they worked. They fired up pro choice or pro life men and women voters. That was another Obama plus.

In the end, plopping Palin on the GOP presidential ticket was worse than a gamble. It was a sure loser. And that even included on the GOP's age old signature issue, abortion.

CHAPTER 17

Colin Powell's GOP Payback

F ormer Secretary of State Colin Powell's endorsement of
Obama was a mere formality. Powell pretty much hinted
that Obama would get the nod from him when he repeatedly dropped glowing and admiring words about Obama
at times during the campaign. Powell's stated motive for breaking
with GOP ranks and endorsing Obama was by then standard stuff.
He'd put a fresh, new, or as Powell called it "transformational" face
on America's much bruised and maligned foreign policy.

There was no reason to doubt Powell endorsed Obama for that
reason. But in another sense his endorsement was a bitter sweet payback for the harsh, odd man out treatment he got from some within
the Bush administration and from others in the GOP.

Despite his impeccable military credentials, unwavering party
loyalty, towering prestige, and diplomatic savvy, Powell always stirred

unease, even deep furor in the bowels of many conservative Republicans. They were never awestruck by the general's bars, commanding personality, and public popularity. That first surfaced when Powell made some soundings that he might seek the Republican presidential nomination in 1996. Pat Buchanan and a strong contingent of conservative groups were appalled.

They sternly warned that they would make "war" on him if he were really serious about grabbing the nomination. If Powell had ignored their threat and charged ahead in his bid for the party's nomination they would have pounded him for backing affirmative action and abortion rights. They would have dredged up the charge that he did not take Saddam Hussein out when he had the chance as chairman of the Joint Chief of Staffs during the Gulf War. The general got their message and quickly opted not to seek the nomination. As it turned out, they hammered him with the soft-on-Hussein charge anyway.

Even so, Reagan, Bush Sr., Gerald Ford, William Buckley and nearly every other Republican big wig were star struck enough with the general's magnetism and perceived popularity that they still wanted him on the Republican ticket. They remembered that in some opinion polls, Powell actually made it a horserace in a head to head contest with President Clinton. They figured that as the party's vice-presidential candidate he could breathe some life into the stillborn campaign of Republican presidential candidate Bob Dole in 1996 while not alienating the party's hard liners.

This was the stuff of delusion. If Powell had actually chosen to run he would have been under the most savage scrutiny of any candidate in American presidential history. The public and press on foreign and domestic policy issues would have mercilessly grilled him. Powell would have been forced to answer the same tough questions and face the same objections as the Republican vice-presidential candidate as he would have as a presidential candidate. And Republican hard rightists would have objected just as strongly to the prospect of Powell being one heartbeat away from the presidency.

The talk of Powell as Republican VP candidate fizzled just as fast as the talk of Powell as presidential candidate did. In 2000, Powell knew that the same Republican rightists still itched to pick a fight with him. He quickly scotched any talk about a Republican presidential candidacy. The Secretary of State post was a much better deal. It gave him a high political profile without the risk of stirring the rancor of the right. As a Bush cabinet nominee, rather than a presidential candidate, Powell would implement, not make, policy. This supposedly kept him out of political harm's way.

But this also proved to be the stuff of delusion. The battle within the Bush administration between Iraq war hawks Vice President Dick Cheney, Secretary of Defense, Donald Rumsfeld and National Security Advisor Condoleezza Rice over the war and the terrorism fight has been well-documented. Powell's diplomacy first tact, his deep understanding that a unilateral too aggressive military policy posed the dire risk of a terrible blowback to U.S. security, and his personal inclinations that Saddam Hussein was largely an impotent, contained dictator who had absolutely nothing to do with the terrorism threat was anathema to the hardliners. They still demanded that he vigorously and enthusiastically help beat the administration's war-drum policy. It was a bitter pill for Powell to swallow, but swallow he did.

He dutifully put a respected face on Bush war doctrine. Even so, he was still closely watched for any hint of deviation from Bush's foreign policy line. This would have brought more howls from conservatives for the general's head.

Powell survived but not without scars. The lies, deceptions, and staggering human cost of the Iraq war that Powell sadly shilled for tainted his legacy of admired, even revered public military and foreign policy service.

Powell's Obama presidential endorsement then was much more than an endorsement. It was the political icing on Obama's campaign cake. It was also a chance to buff a bit of the taint away as well as a nose thumb for past GOP scorn. On Election night, Powell told a CNN interviewer that he sobbed like a baby at the news that Obama had clinched victory. The tears were fitting not just for Obama, but for Powell's GOP anguish. It was payback, if you will.

CHAPTER 18

Overcoming Obama's Blue Collar Blues

A few days before the vote in the Pennsylvania Democratic primary in April, 2008, an audience member at a town hall forum in Scranton shouted at Obama "send them back." The fellow's blunt and grating answer cut through Obama's thoughtful and detailed answer on how he'd deal with immigration reform. A few hours earlier at another forum Obama dealt with the prickly issue of gun control. He gave an equally, thoughtful and detailed answer that straddled the fence between defense of gun ownership and a modified gun control plan. The audience responded with polite but scattered applause. The blunt crack from the audience member on immigration and the modest applause he got from mostly working class whites on the gun issue told much about why Obama initially hit a road bump with many white workers.

It had little to do with race and disgust over Obama's tie to his former race focused Pastor Jeremiah Wright. Immigration and gun ownership were economic and cultural litmus test issues for many non-college educated, blue collar white males. They wanted plain speak not policy wonk nuanced, long winded answers that conformed to their beliefs and views. Obama was learning the painful lesson that plain speak answers on their concerns translated to moral clarity on their concerns.

But it was much more than a failure to grasp the right style and words that caused moderate and liberal Democratic presidential contenders Al Gore, John Kerry and Obama for a time to falter with the majority of white male, blue collar workers. Republicans have played hard on the anger, frustration, and hatred that many of them harbor toward government and the blame they heap for government's perceived failures on liberal Democrats.

The angry white male was more than a cleverly coined buzz word in the 1990s to describe the fear, frustration, and the sense that males, particularly white males, were losing ground to minorities and women in the workplace, schools, and in society. The trend toward white male poverty and alienation first surfaced in the early 1980s when nearly ten million Americans were added to the poverty rolls and more than half were from white, male-headed families. Two decades later, the number of white men in poverty or among lower income wage earners continued to expand. The estimate was that more one in five white males who voted in the presidential election in 2004 made less than $45,000 in household income.

"Liberals didn't realize they had a whole constituency of disenfranchised people without rights who were called standard masculine men," Harvard University social psychologist William Pollack explained. "I'm not saying that all liberal Democrats saw these men as the enemy, but they didn't see them as the victim—but these men felt more and more victimized."

The main culprit in the eyes of those blue collar whites that saw themselves as forgotten, and economically strapped victims was always a big, bloated federal government. It tilted unfairly in spending priorities toward social programs to the detriment of head of household male wage earners and taxpayers.

Though the tax cuts Reagan and later Bush Jr. shoved through Congress benefited the wealthiest taxpayers, they were also the fulfillment of Reagan's promise to deliver mid-America from big government and big spending. It was more than a dream. Reagan delivered on his promise. Reagan cut inflation, boosted employment, and his tough talk on the Soviet Union ("evil empire" plain speak) and terrorism appealed to the simplicity and moral clarity that blue collar workers demanded. Bush Sr., W. Bush followed the Reagan script with mid-America. Bill Clinton did too. He broke the GOP White House stranglehold by masterfully hijacking Reagan's plain speak, emphasis on middle-class pain and the disdain of many blue collar workers for liberals and big government. Hillary Clinton delivered a modified version of that message.

The sense of security and economic boost **Reagan** and Clinton gave to blue collar whites stood in sharp contrast to their feeling Democrats refuse to offer much that will make any substantial changes in their lives. And that they fail miserably to deliver even on the symbolic promises that are made to them.

During the 2004 Democratic primaries, short term Democratic presidential candidate Howard Dean made a clumsy, off-the cuff quip that the Democrats must grab a bigger share of the Confederate flag-waving, pick-up truck driving, gun rack-displaying, white male vote to win. That brought a howl of protest from some Democrats and charges that Dean was a closet bigot from the other Democratic presidential contenders. A contrite Dean backpedaled fast, did his racial mea culpa, and promised to zip his lip on the flag and kowtowing to Southern white guys.

Dean was right. But the rage at him from other Democrats also reinforced the deep suspicion of white blue collar males that the Democratic Party is a hopeless captive of special interests, i.e. minorities, gays, and women, and that white men especially are persona non grata in the party.

The key was finding the right economic formula and words that could overcome the visceral and real hostility to Obama's perceived effete liberalism. The economy was still that key, or rather increasing economic misery and fears among blue collar whites. The economic meltdown in mid September 2008 made things easier. From that point on, Obama stepped up the attack and hammered McCain and his tax policies as a prescription for even more economic misery to blue collar workers especially in hard hit Pennsylvania and Ohio. A win there with their votes would be a sure path to the White House. By November 4th, Obama's message of economic change had done something that Gore and Kerry couldn't do. It struck home with voters in both states. That proved to be the best cure for Obama and the Democrat's blue collar woes.

CHAPTER 19

Not Black President Obama, Just President Obama

The instant Obama tossed his hat in the presidential rink in February 2007 the twin mantra was that he could be the first black to be president and if that happened America had finally kicked its race syndrome. The twin mantra was repeated ad infinitum, and it was dead wrong about Obama and the presidency. The early hint that race was overblown and over obsessed came from Obama. He didn't talk about it. For good reason, he was not running as a black presidential aspirant. He was running as a presidential aspirant. He had to make that crucial distinction for personal and political purposes.

The ritual preface of the word "black" in front of any and every achievement or breakthrough that an African-American makes is insulting, condescending and minimizes their achievement. It maintains and reinforces the very racial separation that much of America claims it is trying to get past. Dumping the historic burden of race on blacks measures an individual's success or failure by a group standard. That's a burden whites don't have. They succeed or fail solely as individuals.

Obama's personal history—his bi-racial parents, his upbringing, his education, and his relative youth—defied racial pigeonholing. He was influenced by but not shaped by the rigid race grounded civil rights struggles of the 1960s as many older whites and blacks were.

The institution of the presidency, and what it takes to get it, demands that racial typecasting be scrapped anyway. Obama would have had no hope of bagging the presidency if there had been the slightest sign that he embraced the race tinged politics of Sharpton and Jackson. His campaign would have been marginalized and compartmentalized as merely the politics of racial symbolism, or worse, racial protest.

He could not have raised record amounts of campaign cash. He would not have been fawned over by legions of Hollywood celebrities, corporate and union leaders. He would not have netted the endorsements of Colin Powell and packs of former Reagan and Bush Sr. administration stalwarts, and been prepped by W. Bush political guru Karl Rove on how to beat Hillary Clinton. The media would never have given him the top heavy favorable coverage, endorsements, nor relentlessly hammered Republican rival John McCain. If the media had so chosen, it could have torpedoed Obama's campaign by playing up his connection with his race focused former pastor Jeremiah Wright. It bought his protest of racial bewilderment at the Wright race revelations, and dropped the matter.

Obama had to cling closely to the centrist blueprint Bill Clinton laid out for Democrats to win elections, and to govern after he won.

It meant during the campaign and would mean at least in the early months of his presidency emphasis on strong defense, the war against terrorism, a vague plan for winding down the Iraq War, mild tax reform for the middle-class, a cautious plan for affordable health care and for dealing with the sub-prime lending crisis, and a genteel reproach of Wall Street.

The old axiom that you can tell a president-elect by his staff and cabinet picks would very much apply to Obama. Immediately before and after his election a cast of governors, senators and ex senators, former Clinton and Democratic party operatives, and even a few to-ken Republican mavericks were floated for Obama's staff and cabinet picks such as Al Gore, Tom Daschle, Tim Kaine, John Kerry, Larry Summers, Robert Rubin, Paul Volcker, Chuck Hagel, Robert F, Kennedy, Tom Vilsack, and yes Arnold Schwarzenegger. The list read like a who's who of the Beltway and Heartland American establishment.

Obama's cautious, center-governing non-racial, likely staff and cabinet cast and policies was plainly designed to allow him to hit the ground running with old, trusted, experienced hands. It was also aimed at blunting the standard Republican rap that Democrats, especially one branded a liberal Democrat, inherently pander to special interests, i.e. minorities, are pro expansive government, and anti-business. They would be watching hawk like for any sign of that from Obama.

The cautious steps were also in part shaped and honed by how he dealt with policy issues during his years in the Illinois state legislature. During the campaign McCain and GOP conservatives slapped him with the tag of the most liberal senator in the Senate and earlier an ultra liberal senator in the statehouse. This was inaccurate and deliberately misleading.

His voting record in the Illinois state legislature gave an early tip of that. He got high marks from liberal groups for votes on environmental, gun control, abortion, civil liberties protections, and ethics reform. But he also deftly ducked taking positions on some of the same issues when they could stir rancor and were potentially polarizing. He voted present (i.e. no position) on bills that would have prohibited a partial birth abortion procedure, reduced penalties for a first offense of carrying a concealed weapon, mandatory prosecution for firing a gun near school grounds, that protected the privacy of sex abuse victims, prohibited strip clubs and other adult establishments from being within 1,000 feet of schools, churches, and daycares, and two parental notification abortion bills. Illinois legislators vote present when they are uncertain or have qualms about some points about a bill. Moderate Democrats in the Illinois legislature vote present when they have reservations about a conservative tinged law and order bill. They worry that by opposing it they would be typed as soft on crime. That would enrage conservatives. Legislators also vote present when they don't want to go on the record against a bill that they oppose. During his stint in the legislature he often used the present vote and rarely gave a reason why.

Whatever his motive for not taking a firm stand on these issues, and not spelling out the reason why, it burnished his credentials with conservative Republicans and right leaning Democrats as a man willing to compromise even conciliate on big ticket issues that conservatives routinely support or oppose.

The most cursory read of his record, as well as a fine comb of his speeches, statements, and interviews, showed that he never claimed bragging rights as the "most liberal Democratic senator." This term was wrongly foisted on him from the start. He was a pragmatic, centrist, Democrat who when circumstances dictated would conciliate conservatives on a hot button issue that might cause political trouble.

As president Obama would be pulled and tugged at by corporate and defense industry lobbyists, the oil and nuclear power industry, government regulators, environmental watchdog groups, conservative family values groups, moderate and conservative GOP senators and house members, foreign diplomats and leaders. They all have their priorities and agendas and all will vie to get White House support for their pet legislation, or to kill or cripple legislation that threatens their interests.

An Obama White House is a historic and symbolic first. However, it's a White House that must keep a firm, cautious and conciliatory eye on mid-America public opinion, and corporate and defense industry interests in making policy decisions and determining priorities. All other occupants of the White House have done that. Obama would do that too and he could not have attained the White House if he didn't do the same. This has nothing to do with race, or the nonsense of being tagged a black president. It has everything to do with the requirement of White House governance.

What to Expect from an Obama White House

President Barack Obama will be the most watched, scrutinized, and perhaps criticized president since Abraham Lincoln. Ironically, the reason for this has less to do with race, though that will loom large in the lens of many, as it has to do with his campaign promise of hope and change. He lifted public passions and expectations to the clouds, and the expectation is that he can repair the shambles of Bush's domestic and foreign policies.

That was quite a cross to bear for a senator slightly half way through his first term. One with a modest Senate legislative record and little experience with foreign policy matters, and whose policy positions on affordable health care, education, criminal justice system reform, tax policy, and the housing crisis were still works in progress during much of the campaign. It was a challenging task for a man who needed to pound consistency into his pronouncements that at times seemed at odds with the other pronouncements he made on winding down the Iraq war and the terrorism fight. But the changes, inconsistencies, and his groping for the right political formula were less important to many supporters than the fact that he was not Bush. The hope remained strong that he would eventually do everything he could to end the war.

The jury will remain out in the early months of his administration on just how many of those inflated expectations that he could fulfill. There were distinct clues as to how much change he could or would make. One was his record in the Illinois state legislature. His votes and views in the Illinois Senate on taxes, abortion, civil liberties, civil rights, law enforcement and on capital punishment gave much comfort to those who crave the change he hints at. His stance on tax hikes marked him with some business and taxpayer interest groups as another tax-and-spend Democrat, and his views on social issues, marked him as an unabashed liberal.

His pro choice and abortion rights defense in the Illinois legislature earned him a perfect rating from the Illinois Planned Parenthood Council. And he was a major backer of legislation limiting police interrogations and requiring police to keep racial stats on unwarranted traffic stops. He also supported strict gun control. These are three hyper-sensitive issues for conservatives. If Obama puts White House muscle into big reform fights on these issues, he will draw instant fire from right to life groups, police unions, and the NRA.

However, he will move cautiously and do everything he can to ensure that the tag "liberal" won't be slapped on him. Centrist to conservative Congressional Democrats and Republicans would instantly draw their line in the sand against him if he makes a quick push for big tax hikes for education and health care to a push for a quick withdrawal from Iraq which Obama does not favor. Liberal Congressional Democrats will move just as cautiously, if only because of the magnitude of the financial and economic morass. That will take up most of their attention, and Obama's too.

Obama will do everything he can to escape the fate that befell Bill Clinton the instant he touched a toe in the White House. Republicans waged a gutter-wallowing personal and political stealth campaign, and at times, open war against him and his policies, and Clinton made no pretense of being a liberal Democrat. Their attack arsenal included everything from personal slander to stonewalling his judicial appointments and his stab at health care reform. That forced Clinton to tip toe even further to the right on the death penalty, beefing up police power, gay rights, welfare reform, and reining in bloated military spending, assuring that the Democratic Party would not pander to minorities and the poor.

It's not likely Obama would risk getting embroiled in the rough and tumble of partisan politics, it's not his style anyway. He got high marks from Illinois Senate Republicans precisely for his willingness to horse-trade, deal-make, and compromise on the touchiest of issues for conservatives. They praised him as a flexible politician and consensus builder who listened to the views of his Republican opponents.

American politics demands that level of compromise, especially of moderate Democrats. With Obama, corporations and lobbyists will be even more hawk like in guarding the legislative door to protect their interests, conservatives will tighten their perennial gate keeping against any effort to push abortion rights, and the defense industry will be even more vigilant against any effort at deep military slashes.

Any president that bucks these dominant special interests risks being branded anti-police, anti-business, pro abortion, pro labor, pro-gun control, and slapped with the dreaded tag of liberal Democrat. This fear more often than not translates into even the best intentioned president carefully weighing the battles he chooses to wage for crucial political and social reforms. Obama more than fits the bill of a well-intentioned president who promises to change the bad, destructive policies of his predecessor. How much of those good intentions he can turn into a reality for America will be the test for the Obama White House.

Hope and Change

In a December 2007 memo and at other points during the presidential campaign W. Bush former political guru Karl Rove ticked off a series of things that Obama could do to win the White House. One thing he suggested was to spell out to voters just who he was and what kind of change they'd expect from an Obama White House. Rove was not simply the proverbial, ethnically insulting Greek bearing gifts. He knew or at least sensed that Americans were fed up to the hilt with the policies of his former boss and his party. They were indeed ready for a change and bought Obama's message of hope.

On the other side Bill Clinton took a beating during the heat of the primaries in January, 2008 for his perceived intemperate and over the top quips about Obama. Yet the advice he repeatedly gave the Democrats every time he was asked how to beat the Republicans worked for him and would also work for Obama too.

In a talk in 2004 to the centrist Democratic Leadership Council, Clinton bluntly told the Democrats to steal the Republican's strong point issues from them. Those issues were national security and defense, publicly downplay social issues, talk up aid to the middle-class, and under no circumstances be perceived as the party that continued to pander to minorities. Kerry followed that script and almost pulled out the election against Bush in 2004. Obama hewed closely to that same script.

He followed the script for other reasons. The American election campaign has never been a straight line affair. There have always been twists, and turns, and occasionally surprises. A slip, a misstep, or a scandal could be fatal to the Republican and Democratic front runners. The Democrats had to be especially wary and guard against overconfidence. They couldn't assume that they could coast to victory over the Republican presidential nominee simply because millions of Americans were disgusted with the domestic policies of Bush and the disaster of the Iraq war. That wasn't enough to insure a victory by Obama. The issues of race, his inexperience, and widespread doubts about his foreign policy fitness were tormenting problems that had to be overcome.

Obama, however, had an organization second to none, record breaking mountain of cash, and a slew of grassroots Democratic leaning action groups such as Move-On. Org that could arouse millions especially young voters, the internet along with Spanish language and alternative radio shows to spin their pitches. He had rock solid black and Latino voting blocs, and, of course, he had Bush's failed policies to take pot shots at.

Obama had one more thing that in the end proved decisive. He had a burning desire to win the White House. That, and the other irresistible political pluses in his column, was how he won.

Notes

Acosta, Jim Acosta, "Democrats dread drawn-out campaign," cnn.com, February 8, 2008

Alberts, Hana R., "Reverend Wright Reclaims the Spotlight," forbes.com, April 28, 2008

Barone, Michael, "How We Pick Vice Presidents," usnews.com, June 29, 2008

Biggs, Matthew, "Black Voters Could swing key states to Obama," Reuters, October 28, 2008

Canellos, Peter S., "Voters signal a loss of patience with president's war plan, Nation signals a loss of faith in war plan," *Boston Globe,* November 8, 2006

Carney, James, "Obama's Bold Gamble," time.com March 18, 2008

Carroll, Jason, "Will Obama Suffer from the Bradley Effect," cnn.com, October 13, 2008

"CBS Poll: Gender Matters More than Race," cbsnews.com, March 19, 2008

Cobble, Steve and Velasquez, Joe, "Obama's Latino Vote Mandate," *The Nation*, November 18, 2008

"CNN transcript of President Clinton's radio address," cnn.com, January 27, 1996

Coile, Zachary, "Vets group attacks Kerry: McCain defends Democra," *San Francisco Chronicle*, August 6, 2004

Cowen, Tyler, "What Does Iraq Cost? Even More than You Think," *Washington Post*, November 18, 2007

Cox, Dan, "Young White Evangelicals: Less Republican, Still Conservative," pewforum.org, September 28, 2007

Crummy, Karen E., "President tall order for Dems in the West," *Denver Post*, March 4, 2007

"Did Sarah Palin Help or Hurt John McCain's Campaign?," foxnews.com, November 5, 2008

Davis Hirschfeld, Julie, "McCain Retools Immigration Stance," AP, February 27, 2008

Duffy, Michael, "Race Spells Trouble for the Dems," time.com, January 14, 2008

Espo, David and Fouhy, Beth, "Clinton grinds out victory over Obama in Pennsylvania," AP, April 22, 2008

"Democrats, Not Bush, Best to Counter a Recession, Poll Says," Bloomberg.com, January 25, 2008

"Exit Polls show sharp divide among Democrats," cnn.com, April 22, 2008

"Exiting Iraq would boost economy more than stimulus," AP, February 19, 2008

Fram, Alan, "Race, gender divide Democratic voters," AP, February 6, 2008

Gelb, Gerald, "Evangelical Power Revives," *Wall Street Journal,* January 4, 2008

Greenburg, O'Malley Zack, "Jeremiah Wright: Barack Obama's Savior?," forbes.com, April 4, 2008

Hendricks, Tyche and Ustinova, Anastasia, "Super Tuesday, Latino Watershed," San Francisco Chronicle, February 7, 2008

Janega, James, "Oprah Helps Raise Money for Obama," Chicago Tribune, October 10, 2008

"Jesse Jackson Apologizes," timesonlone.co.uk, July 10, 2008

Kane, Paul and Weismann, Jonathan, "Latino Community, Female Voters Push Clinton over the Top," *Washington Post,* January 20, 2008

Kaye, Randi, "Some voters say sexism less offensive than racism," cnn.com, February 15, 2008

Klein, Joe, "Obama's Historic Victory," *Time,* January 4, 2008

Macgillis Alec and Agiesta, Jennifer, "For Obama, Hurdles in Expanding Black Vote," *Washington Post,* July 27, 2008

Macgillis, Alec, "No Novelty to Obama's Weakness with Blue Collar Pa. Democrats," *Washington Post,* April 23, 2008

Malone, Jim, "Iraq, Health Care Major Issues in 2008 US Presidential Election," voanews.com, November 1, 2007

McCain Stacey, Robert, "Reviving the Reagan Legacy," *The Conservative Voice,* December 9, 2007

Mellman, Mark, "Can a woman or a black win?" *Los Angeles Times,* Opinion, February 3, 2008

Milbank, Dana, "Joe and Sarah Six-Pack," *Washington Post,* October 2, 2008

Mueller, John, " The Iraq Syndrome," *Foreign Affairs,* November/December 2005

Nagourney, Adam and Halfinger M., David, "Kerry Enlisting Clinton Aides in Effort to refocus Campaign," *New York Times,* September 6, 2004

Newton-Small, Jay, "The Battle for the Latino Vote," time.com, February 1, 2008

"Obama Expects GOP Attack on Patriotism," msnbc.com, June 4, 2008

Ornstein, Norman, "Fight on, Democrats," *Los Angeles Times,* Opinion, February 10, 2008

Page, Susan, "Measuring the nation's mood," *USA Today,* October 14, 2007

Pearson, Rick, "Economy is Voter's Biggest Concern," *Chicago Tribune,* October 21, 2008

"Powell: Why I'm Voting for Obama," suntimes.com, October 20, 2008

Quinn, James, "Real Economy is Biggest Presidential Challenge," Telegraph.co.uk, November 3, 2008

Rend, Jamie, "Can Obama Win the Latino Vote," newsweek.com., Jnuary 26, 2008

"Republicans Debate in Simi Valley, Transcript," *New York Times,* January 30, 2008

Rove, Karl, "How to Beat Hillary (Next) November," *Newsweek,* November 17, 2007

Seelye, Katherine Q., "Did Obama's Speech Reach the Voters he Needs?," *New York Times,* March 19, 2008

"Senator John McCain Defends Iraq War, Bush's Troop Surge Plan, " foxnews.com, April 11, 2007

Schifferes, Steve, "Who Voted for Obama," news.bbc.co.uk, November 5, 2008

Silver, Nate, "Debunking the Bradley Effect," *Newsweek,* October, 21, 2008

Strange, Hannah, "Why Jackson Attack can only help Obama," timesonline.co.uk, July 10, 2008

Sweeton, Lynn, "Powell's Obama Endorsement Undercuts McCain, " suntimes.com, October 20, 2008

Ta-Nehisi, Paul Coates, "Is Obama Black Enough?," time.com, February 1, 2007

Tapper, Jake, "Clinton Launches Obama Attack Website," abcnews.com, December 20, 2007

"The Long Clinton-Obama Seige," Chapter Series, newsweek.com, November 5, 2008

Thomas, Evan and Wolfe, Richard, "Iowa's Field of Dreamers," *Newsweek,* November 12, 2008

Toner, Robin, "2008 Candidates Vow to Overhaul U.S. Health Care," *New York Times,* July 6, 2007

Tremblay, Rodrique, "The Foreign Policy of an Obama Administration," globalresearcher.ca, November 12, 2008

"U.S. President/National/Exit Poll," cnn.com, 2004 Election Final

Van der Gallien, Michael, "Obama Looking Increasingly Centrist," poligazette.com, November 20, 2008

Wallstein, Peter, "McCain has edge over Democrats," *Los Angeles Times,* February 27, 2008

Yaffe, Barbara, "Bush disasters drag down Republicans, Author Argues," *Vancouver Sun,* January 29, 2008

Zucchino, David, "Obama-Winfrey show rolls on," *Los Angeles Times,* December 10, 2007

Index

.

Made in the USA